The Unshakable TRUTH® Journey

GROWTH GUIDES
for Adults

Sacrifice

*Experience
a Deeper Way
to Love*

JOSH McDOWELL
SEAN McDOWELL

HARVEST HOUSE PUBLISHERS

EUGENE, OREGON

SACRIFICE—EXPERIENCE A DEEPER WAY TO LOVE
Course 5 of The Unshakable Truth® Journey Growth Guides
Copyright © 2012 by Josh McDowell Ministry and Sean McDowell
Published by Harvest House Publishers
Eugene, Oregon 97402
www.harvesthousepublishers.com

ISBN 978-0-7369-4343-7 (pbk.)
ISBN 978-0-7369-4344-4 (eBook)

Printed in the United States of America

12 13 14 15 16 17 18 19 20 / VP-NI / 10 9 8 7 6 5 4 3 2 1

CONTENTS

About the Authors

Authors Josh and Sean McDowell collaborated with their writer to bring you this Unshakable Truth Journey course. The content is based upon Scripture and the McDowells' book *The Unshakable Truth*.

Over 50-plus years, **Josh McDowell** has spoken to more than 10 million people in 120 countries about the evidence for Christianity and the difference the Christian faith makes in the world. He has authored or coauthored more than 120 books (with more than 51 million copies in print), including such classics as *More Than a Carpenter* and *New Evidence That Demands a Verdict*.

Sean McDowell is an educator and a popular speaker at schools, churches, and conferences nationwide. He is author of *Ethix: Being Bold in a Whatever World*, coauthor of *Understanding Intelligent Design*, and general editor of *Apologetics for a New Generation* and *The Apologetics Study Bible for Students*. He is currently pursuing a PhD in apologetics and worldview studies. Sean's website, www.seanmcdowell.org, offers his blog, many articles and videos, and much additional curriculum.

About the Writer

Dave Bellis is a ministry consultant focusing on ministry planning and product development. He is a writer, producer, and product developer. He and his wife, Becky, have two grown children and live in northeastern Ohio.

Acknowledgments

We would like to thank the many people who brought creativity and insight to forming this course:

Terri Snead and David Ferguson of Great Commandment Network for their writing insights for the TruthTalk and Truth Encounter sections of this growth guide.

Terry Glaspey for his insights and guidance as he helped in the development of the Unshakable Truth Journey concept.

Paul Gossard for his skillful editing of this manuscript.

And finally, the entire team at Harvest House, who graciously endured the process with us.

Josh McDowell
Sean McDowell
Dave Bellis

What Is the Unshakable Truth Journey All About?

You hear people talk about having a personal relationship with God and knowing Christ. But what does that really mean? Sure, they probably are saying they are a Christian and God has personally forgiven them of their sins. But is that all of what being a Christian really is—being a person forgiven by God?

We are here to say that being a follower of Christ is much, much more than that. Everything you are and what you are becoming as a person is wrapped up in it. When Jesus said he was "the way, the truth, and the life" (John 14:6) he was offering us a supernatural way to follow in his way, his truth, and his life. As we do, we begin to understand what we were meant to know and be and how we were meant to live. Actually, when we become a follower of Christ we begin to take on Jesus' view of the world and begin to think like and be motivated like and live like Christ. And that brings incredible joy and satisfaction to life.

So when we see life and relationships as Jesus sees them, we begin to get a clear picture of who we are and discover our true identity. We begin to realize why we are here and recognize our purpose and meaning in life. We begin to know where we are going and experience our destiny and mission in a life larger than ourselves. Being a Christian—a committed follower of Christ—unlocks our identity, purpose, and destiny in life. It is then that the natural process of spiritual reproduction takes place. That is when imparting the faith to our family and others around us becomes a reality. But what is involved in being that kind of a follower of Christ—a person who has joy and satisfaction in life and knows how to effectively impart the faith to the next generation?

The Unshakable Truth Journey gets to the core of what being a true follower of Christ means and what knowing Christ is all about. Together you and your group will begin a journey that will last a lifetime. It is a journey into what you as a follower of Christ are to believe biblically, how you process your beliefs into core values, and how you live them out in all your relationships. In fact, we will take the core truths of Christianity and break them down into a five-step process:

1. ***What truths do you as a Christian believe biblically?***

    In the first step you and your group will interact with what we as Christians believe about God, his Word, and so on.

2. ***Why do you believe those truths?***

    Sure, you can say you believe certain truths because they are biblical, but when you know *why* they are true it grounds you in your faith. Additionally, it gives you confidence to pass them on to others—especially your family.

3. ***How are these truths relevant to life?***

    In many respects truth isn't very meaningful until you see how it is relevant to your own life.

4. ***How do you live these truths out personally?***

    Knowing how the truth of Christianity is relevant is necessary, but what it leads to is understanding how that truth is to become a living reality in your own life. That's where the rubber meets the road, so to speak.

5. ***How do you, as a group, live these truths out before your community and world?***

    As Christians we are all to be "salt" and "light" to

the world around us. In this step you and your group will discover how to impact your own community with truth that is lived out corporately—as a body.

Be warned! The Unshakable Truth Journey isn't a program to study what Christianity is all about. Simply discovering what something is about has great limitations and ends up being of little value. Rather, this journey is about experiencing firsthand how God's truth is to be experienced in your life right now and, in fact, for the rest of your life. It's about knowing God's truth in a real, experiential way. The apostle John said, "It is by our actions that we know we are living in the truth" (1 John 3:19). You will be challenged repeatedly to increasingly know certain truths by experiencing them continually in your relationship with God and with those around you. It is then you will be able to pass on this ever-increasing faith journey to your family and friends.

There will be two specific exercises that appear throughout these courses. The first is entitled "Truth Encounter." This section is an invitation for you to stop and carefully reflect on the truth of each session. You'll be asked to encounter a truth of God as you relate personally with Jesus, as you live out the truth of God's Word with your small group, or as you relate personally with his people. Please don't rush past these Truth Encounters. They are designed to equip you in how to experience truth right in the room you're in!

The second exercise is an assignment for the week, called "TruthTalk." The TruthTalks are designed as conversation starters—ways to engage others in spiritual discussions. They will create opportunities for you to share what you've experienced in this course with others around you. This will help you communicate God's truth with others as you share vulnerably about your own Unshakable Truth Journey.

What you discover here is to last a lifetime and beyond. You will never finish in this life nor in the life to come. God's truths are designed to be enjoyed forever. You see, experiencing God's truth and knowing him will grow throughout eternity, and your love of him will expand to contain it. And that process begins in the here and now. Your relationship with God may have begun 5 months, 5 years, or 50 years ago—it doesn't matter. The truths explored in these courses are to be applied at every level of life. And what is so encouraging is that while these truths are eternally deep they can be embraced and experienced by even a young child. That is the beauty and mystery of God's truth!

This particular Unshakable Truth Journey is one of 12 different growth guides. All the growth guides are based upon Josh and Sean McDowell's book *The Unshakable Truth,* which is the companion book to this course. The book covers 12 core truths of the Christian faith.

The growth guide you have in your hand covers the truth about why Christ had to die to purchase your salvation. Together in these five sessions we will explore Christ's sacrifice for you and the true meaning of love. Check out the other Unshakable Truth Journey courses in the back of this book.

Okay then, let our journey begin.

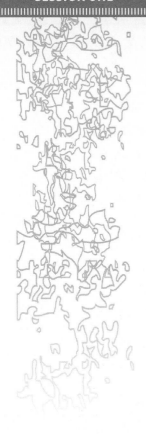

THE HIGH PRICE OF FORGIVENESS

Think of how many times in your life you have said, "I'm sorry" and "That's okay, I forgive you." Giving and receiving forgiveness is a part of life. Identify a time when it was very difficult to say, "I forgive you" to someone who really offended and hurt you.

_____

_____

_____

_____

_____

Why was it so hard to forgive?

_____

_____

_____

_____

_____

Someone read the following.

Forgiveness is about granting relief; giving up a claim for compensation; pardoning; releasing or setting a person free of an offense. And forgiveness does not come without a price. It costs something for us to forgive.

Some time ago a man in Ohio went on a shooting spree and murdered a 27-year-old husband and father. The shooter was convicted and sentenced to die. The widow was at the murderer's execution. The accused gave the longest final statement by a condemned Ohio inmate in memory. During his statement he looked straight at his victim's widow and said, "I am sorry." After the execution the widow was unsatisfied with the man's remorse and said, "It's like I tell my kids: 'Sorry doesn't cut it; you did it.'"

The condemned man said he was sorry and even paid the high price of his own life for his crime, but that obviously wasn't a high enough price as far as the widow was concerned. Sometimes it is very hard to forgive.

Something within our relational DNA wants payment before forgiveness is granted. We have a sense of justice. When wrong is done we want justice to prevail. This sense of justice comes from being created in the image of God. For "God is the Rock; his work is perfect. Everything he does is just and fair. He is a faithful God who does no wrong; how just and upright he is!" (Deuteronomy 32:4). The very character of God is just. When wrong is done he says, "I will take vengeance. I will repay those who deserve it" (Deuteronomy 32:35). The apostle Paul said, "In his justice he will punish those who persecute you" (2 Thessalonians 1:6).

Justice requires payment for wrong done. We have a justice system within states, within the country, and around the world that has established a judicial court system to mete out human justice.

But what about the higher judicial court system of heaven? Can God just say, "Sure, you sinned, but that's okay, forget it—I'll forgive you and we'll be friends"? The reality is that God by nature is holy. He can't just overlook sin. The Bible says of God, "Your eyes are too pure to look on evil; you cannot tolerate wrong" (Habakkuk 1:13 NIV). God is so holy that he "cannot allow sin in any form" (Habakkuk 1:13). So by his very nature he is unable to have a relationship with those infected with sin.

Therefore, even though he is "rich in mercy" (Ephesians 2:4), sin separates us from him. And that separation is a big deal because sin has caused a dreadful consequence: death. The apostle Paul said we "were dead, doomed forever because of [our] many sins" (Ephesians 2:1). Dead people can't accept forgiveness even when it's offered. They can't accept anything, because they're dead. So that presents quite a dilemma. In order for God to forgive us his sense of justice has to address our sin. But just how does he do that?

OUR GROUP OBJECTIVE

To gain a deeper sense of gratitude to God for how his perfect character of justice addresses our sin, allowing him to forgive and redeem us.

God put an amazing and miraculous plan in place in order to forgive and redeem you. Understanding this plan and what it took will enable you to cultivate a deeper sense of gratitude to God.

Someone read Genesis 22:1-8.

Isaac had been taught by his father that there was a price to be paid to obtain forgiveness. A living, breathing creature had to die as a blood sacrifice. Abraham's faith was being tested, but what further was God trying to teach Abraham by asking him to sacrifice his son? How was this sacrifice different for Abraham than other animal sacrifices he had performed before?

_____

_____

_____

_____

_____

_____

_____

Someone read Genesis 22:11-13.

Abraham proved something to God while at the same time making a blood sacrifice. What did Abraham prove, and what blood sacrifice was made?

_____

_____

_____

_____

_____

Someone read the following.

Abraham, like all of us, had sinned and was dead spiritually and separated from God. But in this dramatic example, God was showing him that he had a miraculous plan in place by which Abraham and the rest of us could be brought back to spiritual life in exchange for another life. The ram's life was sacrificed "in place of his son." But it could not be just any life. It had to be a certain type of sacrificial life exchange. There was a certain condition—a criterion required of this sacrifice that was extremely important.

Someone read Leviticus 1:1-4.

What kind of bull was required? _____

_____

_____

Why was the person required to lay hands on the head of the bull?

_____

_____

_____

Why did the bull need to die, though it had done nothing wrong?

_____

_____

_____

Someone read the following.

> The death of a holy and perfectly healthy animal became the substitute for the sinner deserving of death. An innocent life was taken in place of a guilty life. However, the animal sacrifices that God instructed his people to make were but a temporary solution to our dilemma of sin and death. They were only a symbol of what was to come. In order for the consequences of sin (death) to be reversed so we could be made alive to God, a more powerful and perfect sacrifice had to be made.

Someone read 2 Corinthians 5:21, 1 Peter 1:18-19, and Hebrews 2:14-15.

Think back on what the widow whose husband was murdered said: "Sorry doesn't cut it; you did it." Simply telling God you are sorry for your sin doesn't cut it either. Something more is needed. Did Jesus' death "cut it" in God's eyes? Was Jesus a high enough price for God to forgive you? Why?

_____

_____

_____

_____

_____

_____

_____

Someone read the following. (This is drawn from chapter 20 of *The Unshakable Truth* book.)

> Our freedom from the enslavement of sin and death was through the acceptable and redeeming act of Christ as our sacrifice. It was "redemption that came by Christ Jesus. God presented him as a sacrifice of atonement" (Romans 3:24-25 NIV). *Redemption* in this verse is a commercial term. It is a reference to the high price paid to purchase a slave in that day—a price so high that it not only purchased the slave, but also purchased the legal paperwork to buy the slave completely out of slavery. This redemptive price brought total freedom so the person would never again be sold back into slavery. Redemption is the act of Christ freeing us from slavery to sin and death.

The blood sacrifice of bulls and goats was not sufficient or powerful enough for a just God to cancel our death sentence. Jesus, the perfect Lamb of God, was necessary. But his death alone wasn't sufficient either. Something more was needed.

In addition to Jesus' death on the cross, what do you think was further needed to allow God to forgive us of our sins and redeem us?

_____

_____

_____

_____

_____

Someone read Hebrews 9:11-12.

How was our redemption secured by offering a blood sacrifice in the temple before God the Father? Whose blood was it? (This also answers the previous question posed above.)

_____

_____

_____

_____

_____

Someone read the following.

> In mercy and love God the Son died for us.
>
> In justice and holiness God the Father accepts his Son's sacrifice to redeem us.
>
> In power and life God the Holy Spirit declares us righteous and tells us we are his children.
>
> In Jesus we have a sacrificial Savior, Great High Priest, and Effective Defender who sprinkled his own blood in the temple before his Father God "to remove the power of sin forever by his sacrificial

death for us" (Hebrews 9:26). What the priests of the Old Testament did as they sacrificed animals year after year in order to atone for sin was a continuing, ritualistic picture foreshadowing the real sacrifice to come. The true sacrifice was completed in Jesus' final act as High Priest when he "offered himself to God as one sacrifice for sins, good for all time. Then he sat down at the place of highest honor at God's right hand" (Hebrews 10:12).

Therefore:

> **We believe the truth that Jesus, as the sinless Son of God, atoned for our sin through his death on the cross. And the offering of his blood as a sacrifice for sin redeems us so we are forgiven—set free—and raises us to new life in him.**

Truth Encounter

Someone read Hebrews 10:19-23.

The writer of Hebrews summarizes the gift of God's forgiveness and Christ's redemption in Hebrews 10. What if we were to use our imagination to make the truths of Hebrews 10 come alive?

Take the next few moments and imagine the most magnificent, gloriously beautiful throne room that your mind's eye can comprehend. There is a clearly marked crimson pathway that leads to this royal room, and at the room's center rest two brilliantly illuminated thrones: one throne for God, the Father— and to the right, one for Christ, the Son. This throne room is a holy place. Only royalty and those whom the Holy One declares righteous can enter in. This throne room is an intimate place. Only unity and love reside here. Can you imagine what a privilege it would be to enter into such a place?

While you may feel unworthy of such a privilege, is it easy or comfortable for you to accept a seat beside Jesus in this magnificent throne room? Why or why not?

_____

_____

_____

_____

_____

You *do* have such a privilege as a follower of Jesus. You have this honor as one who has been called by him. Reflect on how the writer of Hebrews traces your journey.

Someone read the following and complete the sentence or thought.

- **You have access:** Before your relationship with Jesus, the way into God's glorious sanctuary was closed to you. But now you can have confidence to approach the Holy One. You are now accepted into the throne room. You have access into the presence of Almighty God because _____

  _____.

- **You have intimacy:** Jesus' death opened your access to the throne of grace. Just like the curtain in the Temple, which was torn from top to bottom (see Mark 15:38), Christ's body was torn at Calvary. His suffering and his sacrifice at Calvary opened the pathway to the divine presence of God. You are allowed access to the most intimate of settings because a perfect Priest offered the _____

  _____.

- **You have an Advocate:** And since you have a High Priest who sits on his throne at the right hand of God, you have an Advocate—One who prays to the Father on your behalf. Because of what the Priest has done, you can draw _____

_____ .

- **You have a sacrifice:** On that day when you knelt before the throne and humbly acknowledged your need for Jesus and accepted his gift of redemption, imagine how the Son must have leaned toward you and gently placed his hand upon your head— identifying himself with you—signifying his willingness to _____

_____ .

- **You have right standing:** On that day when you accepted Christ's gift, you were declared righteous; a marvelous exchange took place. In exchange for your sinfulness, you received the Son's robe of righteousness. You can now stand in the presence of the Father, freed from any sense of _____, confident of your standing before God, assured of your _____ _____—all because you wear the regal robe of the Son.

- All of this is freely available because of God's initiative and forgiveness. Jesus paid the price just for _____ !

Spend the next few moments declaring your unshakable hope in the truth of Hebrews 10:19-23 through praise and thanks to God. Consider singing songs of worship. Express your gratitude for what Christ has done for you to one another. Then verbalize your gratitude to God in prayer. Pray with one or two others in your group and express your hope-filled testimony of his faithfulness. Your prayers might sound like:

"God, I am filled with _____ (hope/gratitude/amazement) for how your Son's sacrifice allows me to experience

_____

_____."

TruthTalk—An Assignment of the Week

This week take time to share with a family member or friend what you experienced in this session. Consider saying something like:

1 "I've been learning about the meaning of forgiveness and the incredible price that Jesus paid on

It is Jesus' death on the cross that atones for your sins. He became your sacrifice for sin. His death substitutes for your death, and then his resurrection to life is your resurrection to new life in him. So because of his atoning sacrifice you can be set free, forgiven of your sins, and escape eternal banishment from the presence of God. "For Christ died for sin, once for all, the righteous for the unrighteous, to bring you to God" (1 Peter 3:18 NIV).

the cross. These truths have been so meaningful to me because…

_____

_____

_____

_____."

2 "I've been learning more about some of the ways that Jesus loves us. One of the ways he loves us is that he tells God that he took our punishment for when we do things that are wrong. I am so thankful for that because…

_____

_____

_____

_____."

3 "I've been learning about God's forgiveness—how he 'lets go' of the wrong things I've done because he remembers that Jesus took the consequences of my sin on the cross. That's incredible to me because…

_____

_____

_____

_____."

Read chapter 20 of *The Unshakable Truth* book as a review of this session and chapter 29 for the next session.

Close in Prayer

How Do We Know Jesus Was the Perfect Sacrifice?

Review: How did your TruthTalk assignment go? What was the response?

_____

_____

_____

Have you ever been the victim of a scam? Or have you ever had someone mislead you about something you bought? Share your experience.

_____

_____

_____

_____

_____

_____

_____

> ## OUR GROUP OBJECTIVE
>
> To explore the evidence that
> Jesus of Nazareth was in fact the
> Lamb of God who takes away
> the sins of the world and declare
> that reality before our group.

Someone read the following. (This was drawn from chapter 21 of *The Unshakable Truth* book.)

The worst scam in history or the greatest hoax ever would not compare to the tragic finding that Jesus was not actually the Son of God, the perfect atoning sacrifice that purchased our salvation. Our hope of sins forgiven and eternal life rests in the identity and person of Jesus of Nazareth as the Son of God. And to give each of us confidence and assurance our faith in Jesus isn't a scam or a hoax, God is pleased to give us a clear sign that the man called Jesus is his only Son and Savior of the world.

First, God gave John the Baptist a clear sign to identify Jesus as God's Son. John saw Jesus coming toward him the day after he baptized him and said,

"Look! There is the Lamb of God who takes

away the sin of the world!"…Then John said, "I saw the Holy Spirit descending like a dove from heaven and resting upon him. I didn't know he was the one, but when God sent me to baptize with water, he told me, 'When you see the Holy Spirit descending and resting upon someone…he is the one who baptizes with the Holy Spirit.' I saw this happen to Jesus, so I testify that he is the Son of God" (John 1:29-34).

Just as God gave John a way to identify Jesus as "the Lamb of God," he has also given us clear and indisputable means to identify his Son through what are called *Messianic prophecies*. It is a clear means of knowing with certainty that we can be forgiven by God—because the Jesus of the Bible is our perfect sacrifice.

The information of Messianic prophecy is like giving us a specific address. By looking back to those prophecies we can know if the address is descriptive enough to fit a specific person. And when it does we have no doubt that person is the Son of God.

For example, each of us is one person among approximately seven billion people in the world today. If you were to be identified out of the earth's population, the answers to just eight questions would provide assurance you were who you say you are.

Instructions

Everyone in the group fill in the following. However, some-one read the questions aloud and one person in your group respond verbally.

1. What continent do you live on? _____

2. What country do you live in? _____

3. What province or state do you live in? _____

4. What city, borough, or town do you live in? _____

5. What street or avenue do you live on? _____

6. What is your house or apartment number? _____

7. What is your last name? _____

8. What are your first and middle names? _____

Those correct eight answers just identified a very specific person out of seven billion people alive today. In a similar fashion if we can answer eight questions about the God-man that the Scripture provides as identifiers, then we will know if Jesus fits that identity perfectly.

Someone read the prophecies on the left, which were written hundreds of years before Jesus was born, and someone else read the Scripture passage on the right about the man called Jesus of Nazareth. The question to answer is, "Are those prophecies fulfilled in Jesus?"

1. Out of the stump of David's family will grow a shoot—yes, a new Branch bearing fruit from the old root (Isaiah 11:1).

Read Luke 3:23,31. Does Jesus meet this criterion? _____

2. But you, O Bethlehem Ephrathah, are only a small village in Judah. Yet a ruler of Israel will come from you, one whose origins are from the distant past (Micah 5:2).

Read Matthew 2:1. Does Jesus meet this criterion? _____

3. The Lord himself will choose the sign. Look! The virgin will conceive a child! She will give birth to a son and will call him Immanuel—"God is with us" (Isaiah 7:14).

Read Matthew 1:18. Does Jesus meet this criterion? _____

4. Listen! I hear the voice of someone shouting, "Make a highway for the Lord through the wilderness. Make a straight, smooth road through the desert for our God" (Isaiah 40:3).

Read Matthew 3:1,3. Does this prophecy fit Jesus? _____

5. Rejoice greatly, O people of Zion! Shout in triumph, O people of Jerusalem! Look, your king is coming to you. He is righteous and victorious, yet he is humble, riding on a donkey—even on a donkey's colt (Zechariah 9:9).

Read John 12:14-15. Does this prophecy fit Jesus? _____

6. Even my best friend, the one I trusted completely, the one who shared my food, has turned against me (Psalm 41:9).

Read Matthew 26:49. Does this prophecy fit Jesus? _____

7. My enemies surround me like a pack of dogs; an evil gang closes in on me. They have pierced my hands and feet (Psalm 22:16).

Read Mark 15:24. Does this prophecy fit Jesus? _____

8. You will not leave my soul among the dead or allow your godly one to rot in the grave (Psalm 16:10).

Read Mark 16:6. Does this prophecy fit Jesus? _____

Could It All Be a Coincidence?

Perhaps some of these same prophecies could have been fulfilled in another person of history. Can you identify any other person who fulfilled just one of these prophecies? If so, who?

_____

_____

_____

Anyone in history that also matched all eight prophecies? If so, who?

_____

_____

_____

Someone read the following.

> To date no one has been able to find another person in history that has fulfilled all eight prophecies except for one—Jesus. That means every one of these prophecies was fulfilled during Jesus' life, death, and resurrection. But couldn't that all be a coincidence? Perhaps those prophecies have been fulfilled by any number of people. Right?
>
> This is where the science of statistics and probabilities comes in. Professor Peter W. Stoner, in an analysis that was carefully reviewed and pronounced to be sound by the American Scientific Affiliation,

stated that the probability of just *eight* of those prophecies being fulfilled in one person is 1 in 10^{17}—that's one in one hundred quintillion.

Look at it this way: If you spread 100 quintillion silver dollars across the state of Texas, they would not only cover the entire state, they would form a pile of coins two feet deep! Now, take one more silver dollar, mark it with a big red X, toss it into that pile, and stir the whole pile thoroughly.

Then, blindfold yourself, and starting at El Paso on the western border of the state, walk the length and breadth of that enormous state, stooping just once along the way to pick up a single silver dollar out of that two-foot-deep pile...then take off your blindfold and look at the silver dollar in your hand. What are the chances that you would pick the marked coin out of a pile of silver dollars the size of the Lone Star State? *The same chance that one person could have fulfilled just eight of those prophecies in one lifetime.*

And that's just the beginning! More than 300 prophecies in the Old Testament were fulfilled in *one person,* Jesus Christ—29 specific prophecies fulfilled in one day (see pages 195–196 of *The Unshakable Truth* book). And these prophecies were made more than 400 years prior to his birth! In other words, it is unthinkable to imagine that the Old Testament prophecies about Jesus could have come true in one man unless, of course, he *is*—as he himself claimed—"the Messiah, the Son of the blessed God" (Mark 14:61-62), the One who was and is and is to come.

Someone read John 20:24-25.

Thomas wanted evidence—he said he wouldn't believe Jesus was raised from the dead unless he had proof. Was Thomas wrong for wanting verifiable evidence about Jesus' resurrection? Why or why not?

_____

_____

_____

_____

_____

Someone read John 20:26-29.

What did the evidence of Jesus do for Thomas?

_____

_____

_____

_____

_____

There is indisputable evidence God is pleased to give us that says, "Jesus is the one and only Son of God who came to die and rise again to redeem you." He wants us to check it out like Thomas did. And as you have, what does it prompt in you?

_____

_____

_____

_____

Truth Encounter

Three different people in the group read these passages: 1 John 4:13, 1 John 5:4-5, and 1 John 5:13.

After exploring the evidence that Jesus Christ is the one true Messiah you can now proclaim the same truth as Thomas: "My Lord and my God" (John 20:28).

Your declaration may sound simple, but take the next few moments and share your declaration with one or two members of your group. Speak a few words that declare your belief in Jesus as God's Son. Your response might sound like:

"I believe that Jesus is the Son of God because…

_____

_____

_____."

Now, someone read the promises that the apostle John reiterated for those who believe:

- Because we believe in Jesus as the Son of God, God lives in us and we live in God. We have the opportunity to be close and intimate with Almighty God (read 1 John 4:15).

- Because we believe in Jesus as the Son of God, we have overcome the world. Not only do we have ultimate victory over the world because of our faith in God, we can have day-to-day victory over the influence of this world because of the Spirit's work in us (read 1 John 5:5).

- And finally, because we believe in Jesus as the Son of God, we can be assured that we have eternal life. We can know without question that we will live forever in heaven with him (read 1 John 5:13).

Which of these three promises are most meaningful to you? Tell one or two members of your group why your belief in God's Son is important to you at this time.

"He is my Lord and my God, and I celebrate that he lives in me because…

_____

_____

_____."

"He is my Lord and my God, and I celebrate that I have day-to-day victory because…

_____

_____

_____."

"He is my Lord and my God and I celebrate that I have eternal life because…

_____

_____

_____."

Consider singing songs of worship. Pray together as a group, giving thanks to God for who he is and what he has done for you.

TruthTalk—An Assignment of the Week

This week take time to share with a family member or friend what you have experienced in this session. Consider saying something like:

What extraordinary lengths God went to in order to help us identify and recognize his only begotten Son! Jesus fulfilled 60 major Old Testament prophecies (with about 270 additional ramifications)—all of which were made more than 400 years before his birth. This makes a compelling case for Jesus being the one and only person to "take away the sin of the

1 "I have been learning in our group about how we can know for sure that Jesus is God's Son. I've been so overwhelmed by the truths that…

_____

_____

_____

_____."

2 "I believe that Jesus is God's Son because _____ _____. And I just learned some of God's promises that come as we believe in Jesus. I've been encouraged by the promise that…

_____

_____

world."...God gave us these prophecies so we could be confident in the truth that Jesus truly is God's perfect atonement for our sins.

_____

_____"

3 "The Bible says that when we believe that Jesus is God's Son, God makes several promises come true. My favorite promise is that if we believe in Jesus, we will...

_____

_____

_____

_____."

Read chapter 22 of *The Unshakable Truth* book.

Close in Prayer

JESUS DEFINES THE MEANING OF LOVE

Review: How did your TruthTalk assignment go this week? What was the response?

_____

_____

_____

_____

_____

Love. More books and movies and songs have been written on and about love and romance than any other topic. Identify some notable songs or movies that have made love their theme.

_____

_____

_____

_____

Not all songs, movies, or books depict the true meaning of love. If you were to identify the key markers or identifying characteristics of the true meaning of love, what would they be?

_____

_____

_____

_____

_____

_____

_____

OUR GROUP OBJECTIVE

To gain a deeper understanding of how Jesus defines the true meaning of love and how he became an example for us to follow.

Someone read 1 Corinthians 13:4-5 and Philippians 2:4.

These passages describe some characteristics of love. What are some of those identifying marks of love found in these verses?

_____

_____

_____

_____

_____

Love is other-focused, not self-centered or self-reliant. How did Jesus reflect or live out this kind of love? Give one or two examples of what that kind of love looked like in Christ.

_____

_____

_____

_____

_____

Someone read 1 John 4:9-10 and John 15:12-13.

Real love—Godlike love—does what?

_____

_____

_____

_____

_____

Someone read the following. (This is drawn from chapter 22 of *The Unshakable Truth* book.)

> The cross fell into the hole with a loud thud, sending shock waves of agony through Jesus' legs and arms. Prior to being nailed to the cross he had been beaten almost beyond recognition. Now he hung there on the tree in excruciating pain. Soldiers

below him gambled for his clothes. Religious leaders mocked him. He pushed himself up from his nail-pierced feet, scraping against the rough-hewn cross, in his attempts to get deep breaths. Each time he did this, pain shot up his legs. But he finally managed to draw enough breath to speak: "Father, forgive these people, because they don't know what they are doing" (Luke 23:34). That kind of love is so amazing it defies our understanding.

"God showed how much he loved us by sending his only Son into the world so that we might have eternal life through him. This is real love. It is not that we loved God, but that he loved us" (1 John 4:9-10). The high price for your forgiveness was worth the sacrifice to God. Even when you were an enemy of God, separated and alone, he loved you. He saw your need, humbled himself as a servant, and sacrificed himself for you. That is the true meaning of Christ's love.

Sacrifice reflects Godlike love. Share a time when someone sacrificed themselves in some way to show you love. It could be a parent, a spouse, or a friend.

_____

_____

_____

_____

_____

_____

_____

Someone read 1 John 3:16.

Jesus gave the ultimate sacrifice—his life—for us. But he also made other sacrifices for those around him. What else did Jesus sacrifice to be with his disciples and to give of himself as he did?

_____

_____

_____

_____

_____

We can all think of areas in which we can love others more sacrificially. Without beating yourselves up for where you have failed, share with each other where you would specifically like to improve in demonstrating Christlike sacrificial love to others, specifically your family.

||||||||||||||||||||||||||||||||||||||||||||||||||||||||||||||||||||||||||||||||||||||||

Christlike Sacrificial Love Gives Up Time

Complete the following thoughts and share them with the group.

"I would like to sacrifice more of my time away from _____ _____ in order to be with _____ _____."

Someone read the following.

> What we sense kids are often saying is that love is spelled T-I-M-E. In fact, we all spell love that way. When someone says they love us but don't take the time to be with us, their declaration of love rings untrue. Parents who don't spend time with their kids often make up for it by bringing home elaborate and expensive gifts. But what we want from those we love is not gifts; we want their time. We don't want more stuff; we want the person. Philosopher and poet Ralph Waldo Emerson is credited with saying that a gift is an excuse for not giving yourself. Gifts are important, but they don't replace the ultimate gift of our time.
>
> Some people try to get around the need to spend time with their loved ones by saying it's not the quantity of time that counts but the "quality of the time" that is important.
>
> One of the biggest myths going today is the myth of "quality time." Of course we all want quality moments with our families. But you don't get them by appointment or on some kind of schedule. You

get quality moments by spending larger quantities
of time with your family. Out of the quantity needs
to come the quality. We must have both!

"By spending more time doing _____

_____ with _____ I hope

to enrich the quality of our relationship by _____

_____

_____

_____

_____."

It is not always easy to sacrifice our time, our energy, and our
possessions to meet the needs of others. It requires a love that
is other-focused. And there are yet other characteristics of a
Christlike love that sacrifices itself. What are they?

Someone read Matthew 11:29 and Matthew 26:39.

What further qualities does Jesus' sacrificial love exhibit?

_____

_____

_____

_____

_____

In humility, Jesus yielded to the will of his Father to serve the
needs of others. Jesus personifies the heart of a servant. Why

is that difficult for us to emulate in our own lives? Share openly and honestly why serving the needs of others is sometimes a challenge.

_____

_____

_____

_____

_____

Jesus is the perfect example of one who humbly served others. Christ was not self-reliant, for he relied continually on his Father for strength and wisdom. Christ was not self-centered, for he trusted in his Father and was always focused on meeting the needs of others. And to help us remember how our love is also to come from a heart of a servant, Jesus left us with an illustration to repeat, found in John 13.

Truth Encounter

Someone read Galatians 5:13 and then the following.

The ultimate serving heart of Christ led him to the cross. But his love demonstrated a life of service and sacrifice to others. And perhaps one of the most effective demonstrations or illustrations he gave us was during the Passover meal described in John 13. In fact, he said his illustration was an example to follow.

The exercises that are suggested here may seem different. But what you experience in the next few moments has been practiced in the early church and among many believers for centuries with profound effect. You might want to see this as your opportunity to emulate Jesus as he humbly served others in love.

This requires two volunteers. Obtain two towels, a pitcher of warm water, and a basin. The volunteers are to engage in a visual illustration as the following reading is read aloud. The reader will nod to the two at the asterisk (*) in the reading when to begin. The two will then take turns removing shoes and socks, placing their feet in the basin of water, and allowing the other to gently lift each foot one at a time to dry it off. This should be done slowly and solemnly as the reader reads. When one of the two is done ceremonially "washing feet," they then allow the other to wash their feet.

Begin the reading.

"Before the Passover celebration, Jesus knew that

his hour had come to leave this world and return to his Father. He now showed the disciples the full extent of his love…So he got up from the table…" (John 13:1,4).

What Jesus was about to do not only reflects his servant heart to his disciples, it was a demonstration of what he wants us to be to one another. The act you're about to see represents the meaning of love at its core. It is a ceremony that symbolizes a love that both serves another person and sacrifices for them. It is an act that signifies being with your brothers and sisters in Christ through the good times and bad times, giving them encouragement, carrying their burdens, comforting them, supporting them, and accepting them for who they are. This, followers of Christ, is what Jesus did as an example for us to follow.

*(Now nod to your volunteers to begin. Their action is not necessarily to keep pace with the action described in your reading.)

"So [Jesus] got up from the table, took off his [outer] robe, wrapped a towel around his waist, and poured water into a basin. Then he began to wash the disciples' feet and to wipe them with the towel he had around him" (verse 4).

When he came to Peter, Peter said, "No, you will

never wash my feet!" Peter was like a lot of us—full of self-reliance. Remember, self-reliance is the attitude that says, *I can make it on my own. I'm uncomfortable allowing others to help me. I can do for myself because I can tough it out and grow in my own strength.*

Yet here is what Jesus said to Peter: "But if I don't wash you, you won't belong to me" (verse 8). Instead of humbly accepting Jesus' offer, Peter seemed to go in the opposite direction. Peter said, "Then wash my hands and head as well, Lord, not just my feet!" But Jesus replied, "A person who has bathed all over does not need to wash, except for the feet, to be entirely clean" (verses 9-10).

It was as if at first Peter rejected having his needs met, but then, in self-centeredness, wanted more than Christ designed that he should have. Peter, like most of us, didn't understand that at the center of Christlike love is a "servant's heart." We are to sacrifice (or lay aside) our selfish interests and focus on the needs of others. And so, when Jesus washed the feet of his disciples, he demonstrated his heart to serve and sacrifice.

"After washing their feet, he put on his robe again and sat down and asked, 'Do you understand what I was doing? You call me "Teacher" and "Lord," and you are right, because it is true. And since I, the Lord and Teacher, have washed your feet, you ought to wash each other's feet. I have given you an example to follow. Do as I have done to you. How true it is that a servant is not greater than the master. Nor are messengers more important than the one who sends them. You know these things—now do them! That is the path of blessing'" (John 13:12-17).

Note: Invite and encourage group members to wash one another's feet. Allow God's Spirit to prompt group members to both give and receive during this meaningful time of foot-washing. Consider this experience as an opportunity to give to others (laying aside any selfishness) and receive from others (laying aside any self-reliance). You might consider singing songs of worship and hymns during this time that express your desire to serve and care for one another.

Respond to the following questions after the foot-washing experience:

How has following Jesus' example ministered to you? How has this experience been a living illustration of His love?

_____

_____

_____

_____

_____

TruthTalk—An Assignment of the Week

This week take time to share with a member of your family or friend what was meaningful about this session. Consider saying something like:

Jesus loved us sacrificially, which is why he was willing to come to earth, live with us, and give himself up as our perfect sacrifice. The incarnation— God taking the form of a human—also enabled Jesus to

1 "I recently experienced a special example of God's love. I had the privilege of seeing (participating in) one of the traditions of the early church. I had the chance to serve like Jesus served by washing feet, and I felt…

_____

_____

_____

_____.

experience what we have experienced and be there for us with an affirming love. Christ demonstrated real love for us, and he wants to love others that way through us. When we accept God's sacrificial and affirming love and in turn love others with this same sacrificial and affirming love, we are living out the truth of Christ's real love.

I had the chance to be served by others and I felt…

_____

_____

_____

_____."

2 "In our group meeting I gained a fresh understanding of God's love that is selfless and sacrificial. This experience made me want to…

_____

_____

_____

_____."

3 "Jesus was the perfect example of how to love and give to others. I know he did that well because

_____

_____

and I want to be more like him. This week I intend to…

_____

_____

_____
_____."

Read chapter 23 of *The Unshakable Truth* book.

||||||||||||||||||||||||||||||||||||||||||||||||||||||||||||||||||||||||||||||||||||

Close in Prayer

How to Express Christlike Love to Others

Review: How did your TruthTalk assignment go this week? What was the response?

_____

_____

_____

_____

_____

We've been interacting about how Jesus defines the true meaning of love and how that comes from a heart of service and sacrifice. But is that the kind of love our culture by and large reflects? What are some examples of what the culture communicates to our children about what love is?

_____

_____

_____

_____

_____

_____

_____

OUR GROUP OBJECTIVE

To identify specific ways
Christlike love for one another
is expressed and received and
then love others in that way.

Someone read the following. (This is drawn from chapter 23 of
The Unshakable Truth book.)

"We know what real love is because Christ gave up
his life for us. And so we also ought to give up our
lives for our Christian brothers and sisters" (1 John
3:16). Jesus said, "How true it is that a servant is no
greater than his master. Nor is the messenger more
important than the one who sends him. You know
these things—now do them" (John 13:16-17). Jesus
was our example of sacrificing and meeting people's
needs with a servant's heart. But how can our human
love for others ever match to his infinite love?

Our efforts to love don't compare to God's love any more than a preschooler's coloring book compares to God's multicolored sunset or a hand-molded vase by a pottery maker compares to God's delicate crafting of a newborn baby. Yet his love stands as a pattern to follow, and as we step out in the power of the Holy Spirit to love as he loved, God will empower us to express his love to support, encourage, accept, and comfort as Christ did.

|||||||||||||||||||||||||||||||||||||||||||||||||||||||||||||||||||||||||||||||||||||||||||||||||||||||||||||||||||||

Christlike Love Comforts the Hurts of Others

We all have the needs for attention, affection, encouragement, appreciation, comfort, and so on. Comfort, however, is not always an easy need to meet. For various reasons people oftentimes struggle to serve others in effectively meeting the need to be comforted when life brings us pain and heartache. (*Note:* If you have completed other Unshakable Truth Journey growth guides you may have noticed some of them also include an exercise in giving and receiving comfort. This is intentional. It takes repeated exercises of giving and experiencing comfort to make it part of our lives.)

Someone read the following.

Mary and Martha, two dear friends of Jesus, sent word to him that their brother, Lazarus, was very sick. But Jesus delayed going to see him for two days. And by the time he got there, Lazarus had died.

When Mary met Jesus she began crying. And "when Jesus saw her weeping, and the Jews who had come along with her also weeping, he was deeply moved in spirit and troubled. 'Where have you laid him?' he asked. 'Come and see, Lord,' they replied. Jesus wept" (John 11:33-35 NIV).

Why did Jesus weep? He knew he was going to raise Lazarus from the dead (verse 11). Was he crying for joy? Was he crying to impress the crowd with his compassion? Whom do you think Christ's tears were for?

_____

_____

_____

_____

_____

Someone read Matthew 5:4 and Romans 12:15.

What does Scripture admonish us to do when someone is grieving?

_____

_____

_____

_____

_____

Comfort shares in the sorrows of others. Jesus knew how to comfort people who were hurting. That was part of his servant heart—humbly meeting the needs of others. But many confuse comfort with many other things.

What Comfort Is and Is Not

Comfort means to "ease the grief or trouble of another." So how does comfort actually work? How can feeling sorrowful with someone actually help? Can you explain it?

_____

_____

_____

_____

_____

Someone read the following. (This is drawn from chapter 23 of *The Unshakable Truth* book.)

> For years, I (Josh) didn't grasp the truth of an affirming, comforting love. Whenever Dottie came to me with a problem that she was struggling with, especially one that had caused her hurt, I would try

to fix it. I wouldn't address her pain; rather I would address the problem that *caused* the pain.

One day Dottie came home from a meeting at school very hurt over what some mothers had said about one of our kids. In the past when she shared a problem like that with me, I would leap on the situation and say something like, "Honey, don't let it get to you. Here's what you need to do." Then I would outline a plan to fix the problem. It may have been a good plan, but it didn't address the pain Dottie felt at the moment. But on this particular occasion, I finally got it right. I simply put my arms around her and said, "Honey, I'm so sorry that you had to hear those words, and I hurt for you." That was it—no fix-it plan, no corrective measures outlined, just a heartfelt expression that identified with her pain.

Amazingly, it worked. Dottie felt affirmed, understood, and comforted. And that was all she needed at the moment. A few days later she came back to me and asked what I thought she could do to address those critical comments about the family member. My fix-it plan was then welcomed.

When a person shares in the sorrow of another by hurting with him or her, or identifies with his or her pain, it provides comfort:

"eases the grief or trouble of another." If it were put into a formula it might look like this:

Friend's Sorrow + Your Comfort = Less Sorrow for Friend

Imagine for a moment that you needed the compassionate comfort of a friend or family member. You are hurting, saddened, or grieving in some way. Which of the following responses might ease your pain?

||||||||||||||||||||||||||||||||||||||||||||||||||||||||||||||||||||||||||||||||||||||||||||||||||||||||||||||||||||
Is comfort problem-solving?

"In my opinion, the reason this happened is…"

Why doesn't that approach ease the pain?

_____

_____

_____

||||||||||||||||||||||||||||||||||||||||||||||||||||||||||||||||||||||||||||||||||||||||||||||||||||||||||||||||||||
Is comfort a teaching session?

"In these situations, God instructs us to…"

Why doesn't that approach ease the pain?

_____

_____

_____

||||||||||||||||||||||||||||||||||||||||||||||||||||||||||||||||||||||||||||||||||||||||||||||||

Is comfort a pep talk?

"Come on, cheer up! The sun will come out tomorrow…"

Why doesn't that approach ease the pain?

_____

_____

_____

||||||||||||||||||||||||||||||||||||||||||||||||||||||||||||||||||||||||||||||||||||||||||||||||

Is comfort sound advice?

"If I were you, the next time this happens I would…"

Why doesn't that approach ease the pain?

_____

_____

_____

Problem-solving, teaching sessions, pep talks, and sound advice have their time and place, but not when someone is hurting. Because only comfort "eases the pain."

Someone read 2 Corinthians 1:3-6.

Who is the source of all mercy and comfort? _____

What is one reason God comforts us? _____

_____

_____

When we comfort others with tears of sorrow and a warm hug of love, who is it that joins us in the comforting?_____

Because God is pleased to channel some of his healing comfort through us, we never run short of comfort.

Truth Encounter

Someone read Romans 12:15b.

You can experience Romans 12:15b in the room. This can be done as a group, or you can pair off in groups of two or three. As a group, listen attentively as one person shares his or her painful experience and then other group members provide comfort. If couples pair off, take turns sharing your sad experience and giving comfort to one another.

Share Your Experience

Vulnerably share a sad experience from your past, a recent painful experience, or one from your childhood. For example:

"I remember a time of sadness when…"

Or

"I remember a time when I really needed comfort. That was when…

_____

_____

_____

_____

_____

_____."

Now another provide godly comfort to that person.

- Comfort may *sound* like "I'm so sorry this happened to you," "I feel so sad you're hurting," "I hurt for you and I want you to know I'm here to go through this with you."

- Comfort may *look* like a tender touch on the shoulder or arm, a warm hug, or a tear trickling down a cheek.

Take turns in sharing a sorrow and engaging in Godlike comfort. In doing this you are loving one another with a servant's heart and meeting the needs of others.

Take time to reflect on how God has been pleased to give some of his comfort through you to others. What does this prompt in your heart? Consider a song of praise and thanksgiving.

_____

_____

_____

_____

_____

Truth Talk—An Assignment of the Week

Take time this week to share with a family member or friend what you have experienced in this session, especially how to experience comfort with another. Consider saying something like:

1 "I have recently experienced the importance of loving sacrificially like Christ did. I'm realizing how important and meaningful it is to just listen to someone and show that you care. What I'm learning is…

_____

_____

We can identify with people's sorrow and pain without giving the impression that we know exactly how they feel—which they know is not true. Consider using words similar to these when your loved one is struggling and hurting. "What you're going through must really hurt you, and I want to let you know that I hurt for you. And I'll be here with you." Living out an affirming love brings healing to the pain of another and deepens your relationship with that person.

_____

_____."

2 "I was wondering if there was anything that has been hard for you, sad for you, or difficult for you at school or with your friends. Please think about that possibility, and then I'd like to check back in with you. I want to do a better job of knowing those things in your life because I want to care for you. I won't give advice or try to fix anything. I will just listen and…

_____

_____

_____

_____."

3 "I am trying to do a better job of caring for you—especially during the hard times. Can you think of any sad things or hard things that have happened lately? Let's talk about them because I want to listen and care for you by…

_____

_____

_____

_____."

Review chapters 20–23 of *The Unshakable Truth* book.

||||||||||||||||||||||||||||||||||||||||||||||||||||||||||||||||||||||||||||||||||||||||||||||||

Close in Prayer

DEMONSTRATING LOVE WITHIN YOUR COMMUNITY

Review: How did your TruthTalk assignment go this week? What was the response with those you shared?

_____

_____

_____

_____

_____

Someone read John 13:34-35.

What does our expression of Christlike love prove to your community?

_____

_____

_____

_____

_____

Why does expressing Christlike love among yourselves tell your community you are Christ-followers?

_____

_____

_____

_____

_____

_____

Someone read the following.

> Demonstrating love and care for those around you provides a transparent reflection of Christ. You as a group become a testimony of who Christ is and what he has come to do in this world.

OUR GROUP OBJECTIVE

To plan a group activity that involves demonstrating love and care to one or more groups of people in need of comfort, encouragement, or aid.

In this session you as a group are to brainstorm about an effort to reach out to people in the community to meet their emotional, relational, or physical needs. This could be those who are hurting due to being homeless, without jobs, suffering from the death of a loved one, alone in a nursing home, in need of food or clothing, or in other difficult situations.

Brainstorm: _____

_____

_____

_____

_____

_____

_____

_____

_____

Take the time here to plan your project:

Identify your activity: _____

_____

_____

_____

_____

Set the date and time for your activity: _____

_____

_____

_____

_____

Determine what is needed to execute your activity: _____

_____

_____

_____

_____

Assign responsibilities and tasks for who will be doing what:

_____

_____

_____

_____

_____

Have someone in your group track and record what is being done. This is to record the results of your efforts.

_____

_____

_____

_____

Bring every aspect of your activity before the Lord in prayer.

Someone read Matthew 5:3-10.

As you close in prayer, ask God that he would be honored and praised as you reflect Christlike love to those around you.

_____

_____

_____

_____

_____

||||||||||||||||||||||||||||||||||||||||||||||||||||||||||||||||||||||||||||||||||||||||||||

Assignment of the Week

Execute your activity.

Take the Complete Unshakable Truth® Journey!

The Unshakable Truth Journey gets to the heart of what being a true follower of Christ means and what knowing him is all about. Each five-session course is based on one of 12 core truths of the Christian faith presented in Josh and Sean McDowell's book *The Unshakable Truth®*.

The Unshakable Truth Journey is uniquely positioned for today's culture because it 1) highlights how Christianity's beliefs affect relationships, 2) promotes a relational, group context in which Christians can experience the teaching in depth, and 3) shows believers how they can live out Christianity's central truths before their community and world.

More than just a program, The Unshakable Truth Journey is a tool for long-term change and transformation!

CREATED—EXPERIENCE YOUR UNIQUE PURPOSE is devoted to the truth that God is—he exists, and he created human beings for a reason. It lays a foundation for who people are because they're God's creation, who God designed them to be, and how they can live a life of fulfillment.

INSPIRED—EXPERIENCE THE POWER OF GOD'S WORD explores the truth that God has spoken and revealed himself to humanity within the Bible. Further, he gave us his Word for a very clear purpose—to provide for us and protect us.

BROKEN—EXPERIENCE VICTORY OVER SIN examines the truth about humankind's brokenness because of original sin, humankind's ongoing problem with sin, and how instead to make right choices in life.

ACCEPTED—EXPERIENCE GOD'S UNCONDITIONAL LOVE opens up the truth about God's redemption plan. The truth that God became human establishes his unconditional acceptance of us, which defines our worth. God values us in spite of our sin. This is the basis on which we gain a high sense of worth.

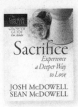

Sacrifice—Experience a Deeper Way to Love digs into the truth about Christ's atonement. The truth that Christ had to die to purchase our salvation shows the true meaning of love—and how God can bring us into a right relationship with him in spite of our sin.

Forgiven—Experience the Surprising Grace of God explores the truth about the power of God's grace. The truth that God can offer us forgiveness in spite of our sin helps us understand how we actually obtain a relationship with him.

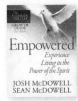

Growing—Experience the Dynamic Path to Transformation speaks to the truth about our transformed life in Christ. The truth about our transformed life in Christ defines who we are in this world and shows how we can know our purpose in life.

Resurrected—Experience Freedom from the Fear of Death focuses on the truth about Christ's resurrection. The truth that Christ rose from the grave and that his resurrection is a historical event assures us of eternal life and overcomes any fear of dying.

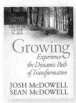

Empowered—Experience Living in the Power of the Spirit covers the truth about the Trinity. The truth that God is three in one and defines how relationships work through the Holy Spirit lays the foundation for how we can experience the power of the Spirit.

Perspective—Experience the World Through God's Eyes examines the truth about God's kingdom and how it defines a biblical worldview. These sessions show how to gain a biblical worldview.

Community—Experience Jesus Alive in His People opens up the truth about the church. The truth about Christ's body—the church—provides us with our mission in life and shows us how to experience true community.

Restored—Experience the Joy of Your Destiny is devoted to the truth about the return of Christ. The truth that Jesus is coming back helps us grasp our destiny in life and gain an eternal perspective on life and death.

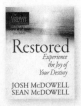

The Unshakable Truth Journey
Sacrifice Growth Guide Evaluation Form

1. How many on average participated in your group? _____

2. Did you read all or a portion of *The Unshakable Truth* book? _____

3. Did your group leader use visual illustrations during this course? _____

4. *Group leader*: Was your experience connecting to the web and viewing the video illustrations acceptable? Explain.

    _____

    _____

5. On a scale of 1 to 10 (10 being the highest) how would you rate:

    a) the quality and usefulness of the session content? _____

    b) the responsiveness and interaction of those in your group? _____

6. To what degree did this course deepen your practical understanding of the truths it covered?

    ❏ Little   ❏ Somewhat   ❏ Rather considerably

    Please give any comments you feel would be helpful to us.

    _____

    _____

    _____

    _____

Please mail to: Josh McDowell Evaluation
                 PO Box 4126
                 Copley, OH 44321